Help Me; I'm Lost

by Christine Kohler
illustrated by Keith Neely

Concordia Publishing House
St. Louis

Scripture quotations are from The Holy Bible: NEW INTERNATIONAL VERSION, ©1978 by the International Bible Society. Used by permission of Zondervan Bible Publishers.

Copyright ©1985 Concordia Publishing House
3558 S. Jefferson Avenue, St. Louis, MO 63118-3968
Manufactured in the United States of America

All rights reserved. No part of this publication may be reproduced, stored in a retrieval system, or transmitted, in any form or by any means, electronic, mechanical, photocopying, recording, or otherwise, without the prior written permission of Concordia Publishing House.

Library of Congress Cataloging in Publication Data

Kohler, Christine, 1953-
    Help me, I'm lost.

    (Growing up Christian series)
    1. Children—Religious life. I. Title. II. Series.
BV4571.2.K64 1985   248.8'2   84-22952
ISBN 0-570-04115-5

1 2 3 4 5 6 7 8 9 10 DB 94 93 92 91 90 89 88 87 86 85

It was a hot, lazy, end-of-summer day when Scotty burst through the kitchen screen door.

"Mommy, Mommy! There's gonna be a festibal. A festibal with real firemen and clowns and everything! Curtis' mom says so. Can we go? Please, can we?" Scotty asked excitedly.

"It's a *festival*," laughed Mrs. Harper. "The Firemen's Festival; and, yes, we are going. I told Mrs. White we would take Curtis with us because Mr. White is a volunteer fireman and they are both going to work at the festival."

Jennifer walked into the kitchen carrying two sweaters.

"Jenny, we're going to a festi...festival!" said Scotty. "With firemen and clowns and everything!"

"Are we really, Mom?" asked Jennifer.

"Yes, we are going to a festival this weekend before school starts. The volunteer fire department is having a fair to raise money to buy a new firetruck."

"Hooray!" shouted Jennifer and Scotty together.

"Here are the sweaters you wanted, Mommy," said Jennifer.

"Thank you, Jennifer. Just put them on the table, please." Mother was busy hunting in the cupboards for the lunch boxes.

"Hey," said Scotty, "that's my favorite sweater. It's too hot to wear it now."

"You're right, Scotty, it is too hot to wear now. But in another month or so the weather will cool down, and you will need the sweater for school," explained Mother. "Ah, here are the lunch boxes!"

"Yea!" cheered Scotty. "I like my red lunch box with the pictures of horses on it."

"I like mine, too," said Jennifer, "but sometimes I'd rather buy lunch at school instead."

"Maybe, sometimes you can, Jennifer. But, just in case, I need to make sure everything is ready for school," said Mother. "Now, Jennifer, would you please get me your new backpacks and school supplies?"

"What are you going to do with all of our school stuff, Mommy?" asked Scotty. "Do we go to school tomorrow?"

"No, not until next week. I need to write your names in everything so if it gets lost and someone finds it, they will know who it belongs to."

"Can I help?" asked Scotty.

"As a matter of fact, yes. Practice printing your name, address, and phone number on this piece of paper." Mother got a piece of paper and pencil and printed:

    Scott Michael Harper
    1525 Elm Street
    533-7212

"Do I have to?" asked Scotty. "I want to go play."

"Yes, you have to," said Mother. "You need to know your name, address, and telephone number before you start school. Since you are growing up, there will be times when you won't be with Daddy or me."

"Like at school?"

"Like at school, on the bus, or at the library," added Mother. "And if for some reason you should get lost, you would need to know your name, address, and phone number to tell a grown-up. After you've learned to write them, I am also going to teach you how to dial our number on the telephone."

"Oh, boy!" shouted Scotty. "I get to use the telephone. I'm gonna learn this real quick!"

Jennifer brought in the new backpacks and school supplies.

"What did you say about getting lost?" Jennifer asked.

"I was just telling Scotty what to do in case he gets lost," said Mother.

"We had a story in Sunday school last Sunday about a man who lost a sheep," said Jennifer. "My teacher said we are like sheep and Jesus is our Shepherd."

"A shepherd is a sheep-keeper," declared Scotty.

"A shepherd takes care of the sheep," replied Jennifer.

"Same thing," said Scotty, "A sheep-keeper!"

"Anyways, Jesus said this man had a hundred sheep and one got lost, so he left the ninety-nine sheep to go find the one."

"Did he leave a sheepdog to take care of the rest of the sheep?" Scotty asked.

"I don't know," replied Jennifer, "the Bible didn't say."

"I'll bet if he had had a good sheepdog he wouldn't have lost the one sheep in the first place," said Scotty.

"Go on with the story, Jennifer," urged Mother.

"Then Jesus said, when the man found the lost sheep, he was happier with that one sheep than all the others that didn't get lost."

"I know that memory verse!" shouted Scotty. "'I have strayed like a lost sheep;' Psalm 119:176."

"Very good, Scotty," praised Mother.

"But that wasn't it," said Jennifer. "It was, 'The Son of Man came to save what was lost;' Matthew 18:11."

"That was an appropriate story, Jennifer," Mother said.

For the rest of the afternoon Jennifer helped Mother tag everything with their names while Scotty practiced saying and printing his name, address, and phone number. Best of all, he liked dialing the telephone.

The week passed by quickly as they prepared for school to start. Mrs. Harper walked Jennifer and Scotty to the bus stop to make sure they knew exactly how to get there. Mr. and Mrs.

Harper drove Jennifer and Scotty to school to help them find their new classrooms and meet their teachers. At the end of the week Mrs. Harper made a big cherry cake with pink frosting for the bake sale booth at the Fireman's Festival where Mrs. White was working.

Saturday morning Jennifer and Scotty were so excited about the festival that they got up extra early.

"Oh, boy!" said Scotty. "I can hardly wait until the festival starts."

"Me, too," said Jennifer. "I want to ride on the Ferris wheel and go up real high."

"Not me," said Scotty. "I want to see the firemen and clowns and everything first!"

"I'm glad my best friend Curtis gets to come with us," said Jennifer.

"I'm glad Curtis' daddy is a fireman," said Scotty.

At the Firemen's Festival there was excitement everywhere. People from all over had come to enjoy the amusement rides, play games, and see the fire engine display. There were so many rides to choose from: boats with little bells that bobbed around in a circle in the water; the big Ferris wheel that took you high in the sky; a small roller coaster that wasn't too scary; and a splendid merry-go-round with horses. And all in a row sat a line of game booths. There was a fishing booth, a pop-the-balloon-with-a-dart game, a bean bag toss game, plus much much more.

And the food! There was a big open tent with tables where they served hot dogs, hamburgers, chicken, and french fries. There were booths for cotton candy, candy apples, snow cones, and the bake sale.

Best of all was the display with lots of fire engines. Men with firemen uniforms and hats were showing everyone the antique fire engines and the new fire engines. One man was showing a film about fire safety.

There was so much to see and do that Jennifer and Curtis and Scotty wanted to run in all directions and do it all at once.

"Now let's all hold hands and stay together so we don't lose anyone," said Mr. Harper.

"I don't want to hold Jennifer's hand!" said Scotty.

"Then you can hold mine, Scotty," said Mother. "Just stay close to us."

"I want some cotton candy and a balloon and a ride in the little boat!" said Scotty excitedly.

"All at once, I suppose," laughed Father.

"Daddy, please take us up in the Ferris wheel," begged Jennifer.

"I don't like the Ferris wheel," said Scotty. "I'm scared when it stops at the top."

"Well, Daddy can take Jennifer and Curtis on the Ferris wheel and you and I can wait down here for them. Then you can go on the boats next," suggested Mother.

Mr. Harper and Jennifer and Curtis got on the Ferris wheel. Their seat swung back and forth. Their seat went up, up, up, over the top, then down again. Mother was busy watching Jennifer and Curtis. She would wave and call to them as their seat would go down, down, around in front of her.

Scotty was upset. He wanted to get cotton candy and a balloon and ride on the boats *now*. Just then Scotty saw a clown go by giving out balloons to children.

"I want a balloon, too," he thought. Scotty ran after the clown without telling his mother. The Ferris wheel stopped. Mrs. Harper reached down to hold Scotty's hand again. Scotty was gone!

"Scotty," called Mother. "Scotty Michael, where are you?"

Father appeared with a happy Jennifer and Curtis.

"What's the matter?" Father asked.

"I let go of Scotty's hand for just a minute and now he's gone!" said Mother. "Where could he be? I told him to stay with me!"

"Don't worry," said Father. "We'll find him. You stand here for awhile with the other children in case he returns here and I'll go look for him."

"Mommy," said Jennifer, "Scotty is like the lost sheep. I'm going to pray Jesus helps us find Scotty."

"I'm going to pray with you," said Curtis.

"That's a good idea," agreed Mother.

Mrs. Harper tried not to worry, but to trust Jesus to keep Scotty safe and help them find him. The minutes dragged as she waited by the Ferris wheel with Jennifer and Curtis. Suddenly there was a voice on the loudspeaker asking if the parents of Scotty Harper would please come to the information booth.

"They must have found Scotty. Let's hurry!" said Mother.

Scotty was standing at the information booth looking very sad. He knew he had done the wrong thing by running after the clown. When Mother saw Scotty she was both mad that he had disobeyed and glad that he was found.

"I'm sorry I didn't listen to you, Mommy. I'm sorry I ran after the clown with the balloons," wailed Scotty.

Mother reached down and gave Scotty a big hug. "I am just so relieved that you were found."

Scotty's face brightened. "When I ran so far and couldn't see you anymore, I got real scared. But then I remembered what you told me to do if I got lost, so I went up to a fireman and told him my name and address, and phone number, too. Then he brought me here."

"You did the right thing, Scotty," said Mother.

"Where's Daddy?" asked Scotty.

"Oh, my! He's still out looking for you, and now that we have left the Ferris wheel he won't be able to find us, either." said Mother.

"Then we better make a 'nouncement: 'Daddy,
If you're lost, we're found. Come and get us,'"
said Scotty. "And I'll even hold Jennifer's hand...
if I have to!"